INDIAN TERRITORY AND OTHER POEMS

by H. L. Van Brunt

UNCERTAINTIES

INDIAN TERRITORY AND OTHER POEMS

Indian Territory and Other Poems

by

H. L. Van Brunt

With drawings by Jim Kay

THE SMITH
by arrangement with Horizon Press
New York 1974

Copyright © 1974 by H. L. Van Brunt
All rights reserved
First Edition
Library of Congress Catalog Card Number: 13-6164756
ISBN: 0-912292-32-6

Grateful acknowledgement is made to the following publications
in which these poems were first published:
The Arlington Quarterly, The Arts in Ireland, December, Gnosis, Hearse, The Kansas City Star, The Kansas City Times, Latitudes, The Literary Review, The New Orleans Review, The New York Times, Red Cedar Review, The Smith, The South Dakota Review, Southwest Review, Twigs, The Unspeakable Visions of the Individual, and *West Coast Review*
Some of the poems have been revised since their initial publication

**Printed in England by Villiers Publications Ltd
Ingestre Road, London NW5**

for laura, al & harry

CONTENTS

Indian Territory

11	BLOOD OF THE LAMB
13	DEATH OF THE INDIAN CARPENTER
15	ON THE PRAIRIE
16	LION
17	THE SPRING
19	RUNNING TOWARD THE SUN
21	ON THE DEATH OF C. B. REYNOLDS
23	THE HOMECOMING
25	MORNING
26	JOURNEYS
27	DROWNING
28	BIRDS IN HAND
29	A WALK BEFORE DINNER
30	GOING HOME
31	MELTING
32	THE CITIZEN

The City, The Sea & The World

35	THE GIFT
36	A CHRISTMAS POEM
37	LEGEND
38	MINSTREL
40	WALKING
41	CHINA BLUE
43	THE IMAGE
45	THE BURGLAR
46	PETRELS
47	THE FORAGERS
49	THE HEIR
50	MEMOIRS
52	IN THE OSTERREICH

54	DECEMBER LETTER TO NINA
55	SNAPSHOT
57	LAKE/MAN/BIRD
59	POEM FOR THE PEOPLE OF YOUGHAL

Indian Territory

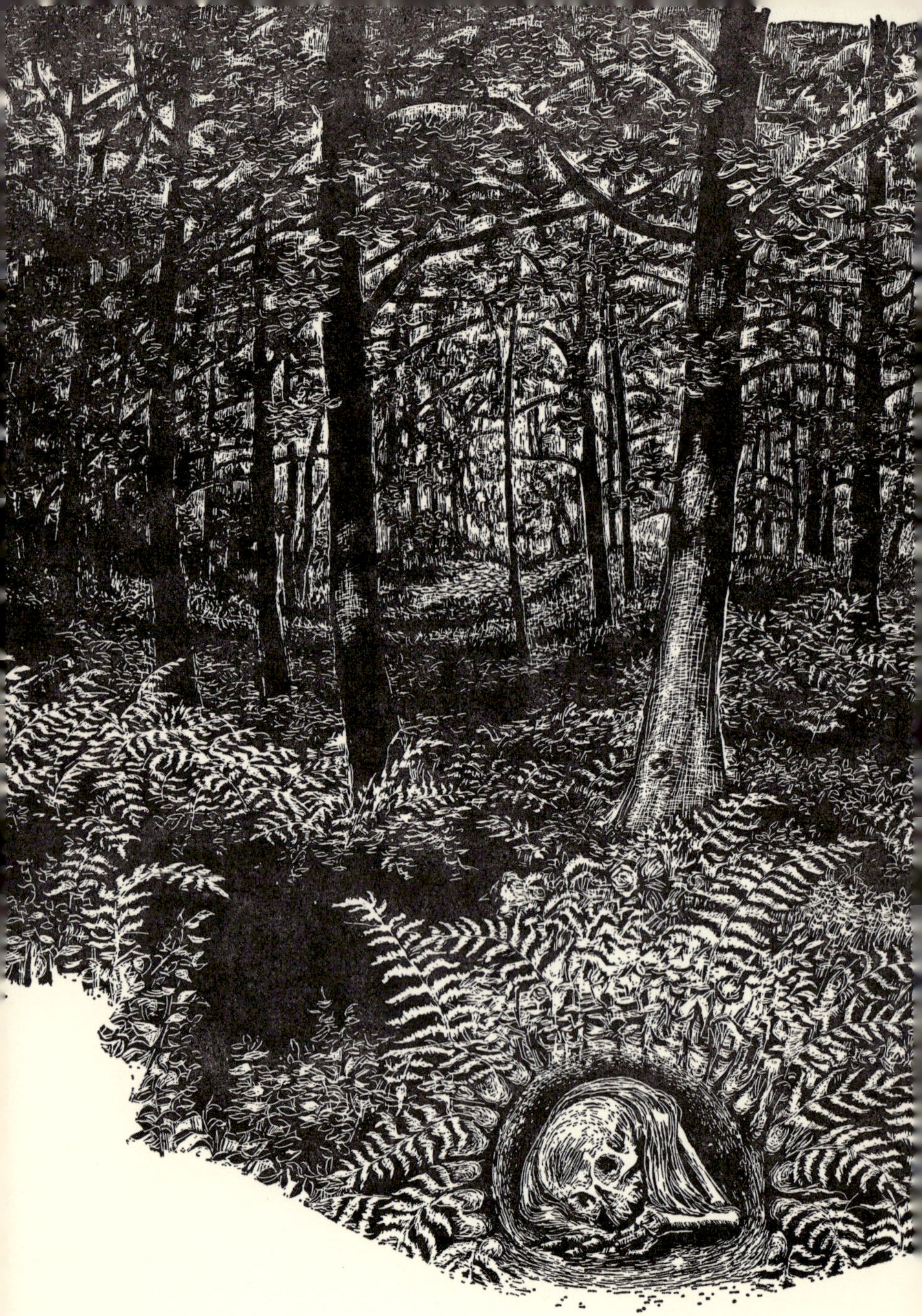

Blood of the Lamb

1.

i see you
sister said
tongue consistency of a cat's

watching me come all over
some technicolored
ass

my sister's mouth would have held the moon
her eyes
were innocent as doris day's

("my hair's
as blonde
as hers")

2.

my family have died like poets for generations
moving to their own rhythm
new york to tennessee

tennessee to oklahoma
farmers, carpenters, whisky-makers
liars, thieves & soldiers

bad lungs & pride
in a queer dutch name
their only legacy

bragging they were barons of new york
when the puritans slept
with the indians

3.

my sister died
coughing & laughing & smoking lucky strikes
in a hospital on the prairie

Death of the Indian Carpenter

the timber rattler's head
swung heavy as a plumb
into your log-thigh

....

the buck you didn't kill
beds down on a rise

warm breath, and belly full
as the harvest moon
that's red on the window

of the tahlequah funeral home
& shines in his eyes

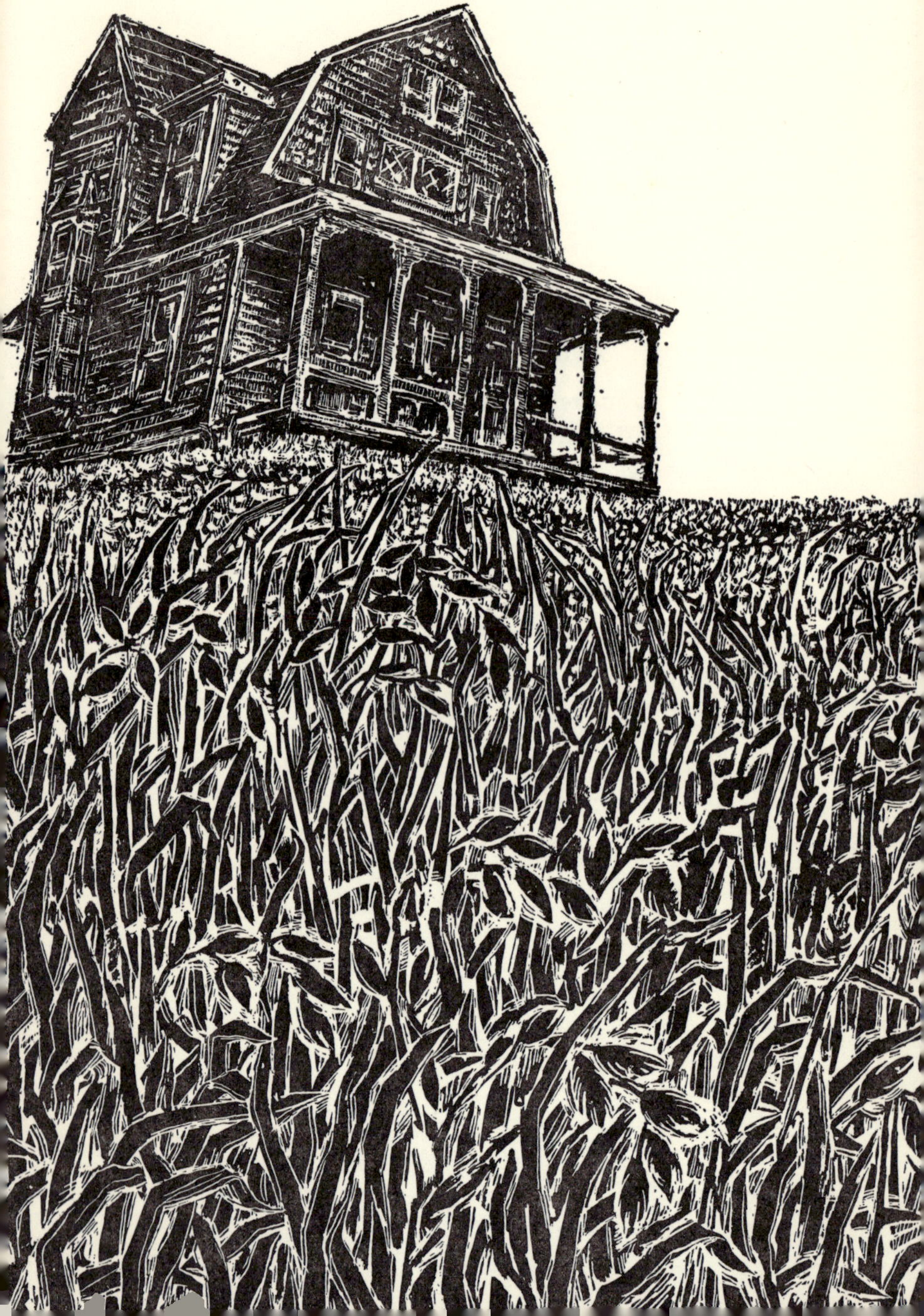

On the Prairie

The house leans back
like an old man
fallen asleep in the waning sun.
A porch plank lifts
a rusty nail.

No one lives here now.
No other house for miles.
Nothing but yellow grass
and sandstone,
keeping quail company.

Lion

Old man, your face is like the moon's
topography — valleys, mountains, rivers
cracked and dry.
The side you never show
darkens in your eyes.

In the cave of this old house
your room's the den you'll die in.

Smelling of Vaseline
your life's compressed
to rags of memory.
They'll sweep you out with the dust —
wrapped in Police Gazettes.

The Spring

The sky wore clouds
the way the marshal
wore his hat.
He kept telling us that
we'd like it there.
Movies twice a week,
and school
right on the premises.
His eyes were hidden as the sun.
The highway ran through the trees like a trail.

My sisters always liked the spring.
They built their dollhouse there.
The black
water spilled
into the creek
by its own weight.
We sat on the leaves like Indians,
tossing pebbles at the waterbugs.

They sat us down in a room like a shed.
The woman urging us to eat
was big as a house, or a hall, or the world
that placed us there. But in our eyes
she disappeared.

I hardly write to my sisters now.
They remind me of the matron
that slapped us till we ate.

Only the one who died has eyes
the color of the spring,
and arms loose as leaves.

Running Toward the Sun

you kindle my sleep
O enormous eyes
in a small ship's frame
I touch your heart
you die

Yes, I will take care of my brother.
(Remember I memorized the Bible,
was called to recite verses in front of the class,
and stood bewildered and hated and wondered
what was wrong.)
I promise you that.
Please sleep
in your dirt bed.

O you who never relented
who never gave anything up to the world
your small fists
failed

Elva, Elva, Cherokee-Swede
Doomsayers all
haunting the grave
as though they had never been alive

Alive to see a girl walk over the grass
twenty summers ago — flower-frail.
I'll take my children back, you said.
We ran toward the sun,
away from matrons, and the mass
of the unloved, and orbited.

But O we let you go.
We saw your suffering as a sign . . .
or curse on us, and cursed you for it.
We lived in the real world
where love doesn't cure anything at all,
where staring children swear to get even
for everything you couldn't give.

And who let you die alone.
Who wears the emblems of the sun.
And who will die himself alone
as a young or an old unlovely man —
crying for his mother,
and love that does not return.

On the Death of C. B. Reynolds

Something fumbles at the latch.
The sleeping man yells *hey! hey! hey!*
Over and over —
Flopping like a fish
In a huge palm.

I remember you for what you weren't.
How easily authority sat upon you —
The sense of a man who knew his place —
And with what rightful wrath
Authority came down.

I wonder if you went down to death
With the same sense of place.
If, for a moment, you lost trust
In the ways of the Lord.
Certainly you admitted they were strange.

Charles Bryan Reynolds, I could say
You had been conned, and put upon
All of your natural life —
That the men you idolized
Shat in much the same way as you —

That dreams you had (finding gold
On that old farm; becoming an actor ...
From usher at the Wichita Paramount;
Finding Valhalla in New Mexico)
Were cheap, not worthy of your soul.

But you were selfish. You reserved
The best you had for your own senses.
The leanest porkchop, the biggest eggs
Went on your plate. Humbly we watched
You deliberate.

"Spell 'black,' " you said; I couldn't; watched
You down in wolfish bites my cake.
"B-l-a-c-k," you said.
Turning to mother,
"He don't seem so smart to me."

Always that set of horseteeth taunted:
"Don't fall down — Mama'll cry."
"Blockhead" was the favorite epithet
You spat, and the bedsprings creaked a little louder
Nights after days we had arguments.

Charles Bryan Reynolds — Born, August, 1899,
Indian Territory. Dead, April, 1969,
The New Orleans Veterans Hospital,
Of tuberculosis — following mother
By a year — I wish you well.

And ask your forgiveness of my hate;
And for not wanting to be an actor
Or dreaming of New Mexico
I offer this, to expiate:
To mine the gold on the farm of my father.

The Homecoming

Fires on the mountains,
night winds, the drift of seas
are all the same to me —
my home is in my head.

Grass and earth report
nothing I do not know —
not dissonance of trees,
or semaphores of snow.

Whales going home
follow in my wake.
Venus charts our courses.
We move for our own sakes.

Journeys never ending,
lives never begun
relate themselves as wind
and prairie grass become

a hymn in praise of nothing
... the way
things work under the sun.
We are like the clouds,

that change from sky to sea.
It is, as I have said,
all the same to me.
My home is in my head.

Morning

nothing is more silent than a star
except a heron
standing at the water's edge
neck cocked like a gun

Journeys

The conversations of the leaves
Turn to silence on the river,
And in that silence reigns the sun,
And in those legions of the leaves,
As they strike against their neighbors,
The wind sows the secrets of the sun.
In several tongues and several voices
Leaf-choirs begin to separate,
Their deaths now individual
As they journey to the woods
That lie in the next world.

Drowning

placing stones sweet as chocolates
on the graves of emperors
i move

my hands through the light
bridges
to the dark below

one-half of me is black
and one-half white
i hold

the water to my breast
as though it were the child
of my life

Birds in Hand

You seem to recede when you go to sleep.
Something about you evades the light.
When I cup your hips in my hands
I am entering the world.

They say you are cold, but I don't believe it.
That's just your way of being polite.
You tell men what you think of them in bed —
Where it counts, and doesn't have to be said.

Your body speaks many languages.
Lips proclaim your liberality.
And I sing like a bird
In the foliage of your limbs.

A Walk Before Dinner

Something drops out of the leaves
on something else.
Owl on fieldmouse.

I do not even hear the small scream
or the heavy wings beat back to the tree,
or fix the position of the moon

above the dark cloudbanks.
But walk the river, where luminous rafts
of mosquitoes float silently by,

and tree shadows hang in the water.
Smoking, I hear
an occasional fish

make a splash.
But mostly the quiet air breathes
on my cheek,

and makes me hungry.
My wife should have on the table
the old hen whose head I wrung off today.

Going Home

My line is lifted
from the water
by an evening breeze.
Darkness walks
along the river
like the shadow
of a man.

I have caught
carp all day.
No bass, no catfish,
no large perch.
Some thoughts of you.
I shall loose the carp
to their dark home.

Melting

The moon breaks
through the window
of this greenhouse

called a room.
Tendrils drag
across my face.

Night
is a pimp with wornout whores
that I have slept with countless times.

The bare tree
rises, with the wind
for leaves.

The moon,
confessor to the night,
is near and far

as God. Murders
break out of my head.
Asleep

I rape the world.
I have forgotten
everything I learned.

The Citizen

So, of course, being law-abiding,
recently moved from the country, and awed
by the machinery of the government
I even helped them lift the dog
into the van —
saw him cower
and look down
(who had only held the arm
of some kid who hit my sister).

Now, of course, I'm full of theories —
discussing Hegel, literature,
revolution, Che Guevara —
but in my gut I know I am
that ignorant, sixteen-year-old coward,
too dumb to know of licenses,
who helped a bunch of
sons-of-bitches
murder what he loved.

The City, The Sea & The World

The Gift

In the basement, boxes tied,
neat as the bun of her hair.
"Three days ago I called
and now you finally come."
Standing by the door,
she calls; there is something more,
brighter than the light.
A knife curved like a scimitar,
eased into its sheath,
proffered handle first.

"My boy's. He made it.
Ugly thing. Keep it or
throw it away."
She waves and
shuffles back
to her house among the trees.
I step through beds of leaves
draining on the lawn
with the oiled
blade of her son.

A Christmas Poem

A woman staggers along the street,
talking to everyone she meets,
trying to explain her life.
Now she is pulling off her clothes,
but no one bothers to listen
even to this baring
of her soul.

She will wake in jail,
and add another blotch to the spreading
                                bruise that is her life.

Haze has settled on the city.
Sunday morning
turns in the distant sky.
All human blood revives
to sing hosannas to the sun —
in whose light it gushes, with good cheer,
from our images.

Legend

clouds like long, black veils
bandage the sky

the river's so black tonight
the dead must get lost

perhaps they sit like owls
huddled in the trees

that run in lines across the city
waiting for the sky to clear

Minstrel

in the nest of his shoulders rode
toucans, parrots, and a hummingbird
trilling out his life
in arias of alcohol

the cave of his stomach was filled with the small
bones of women
the green
edges of his head had turned to cheese

blue tide rising from the edge of the sea
birds that gather
in the skies
listen to me

he did not like to touch dead things
or fill his mouth with shadows
but wanted the red flag of his tongue to fly
over meadows

and hold what he held dear beside him
and listen to the words of water and wind
blades of grass were his cold children
but you were indifferent as his eyes

that faced the grey faces of the streets
and flew no flags but those of wine
a bottle smashed in either hand
as he was hit   now sing GODDAMN!

Walking

I sing the body electric . . . — Whitman

Trees with
leaves of rain
shine
down long rows of streets.
Footsteps pound. From heels a curious
surging of the nerves
floods in steady shocks. Hands
feel electric. Eyes
glow more than a cat's. Body,
organic as a tree,
with perfect faith in molecules,
would walk to the end of the world —
singing blood's syllables.

China Blue

for Laura

Clouds like
bruises bloom
on the sea at Montauk.

Today was china blue.
Clouds became the sand
between our toes.

We stared,
our lives like the days of wasps
without a nest.

We stared,
our lives
larval in the sea.

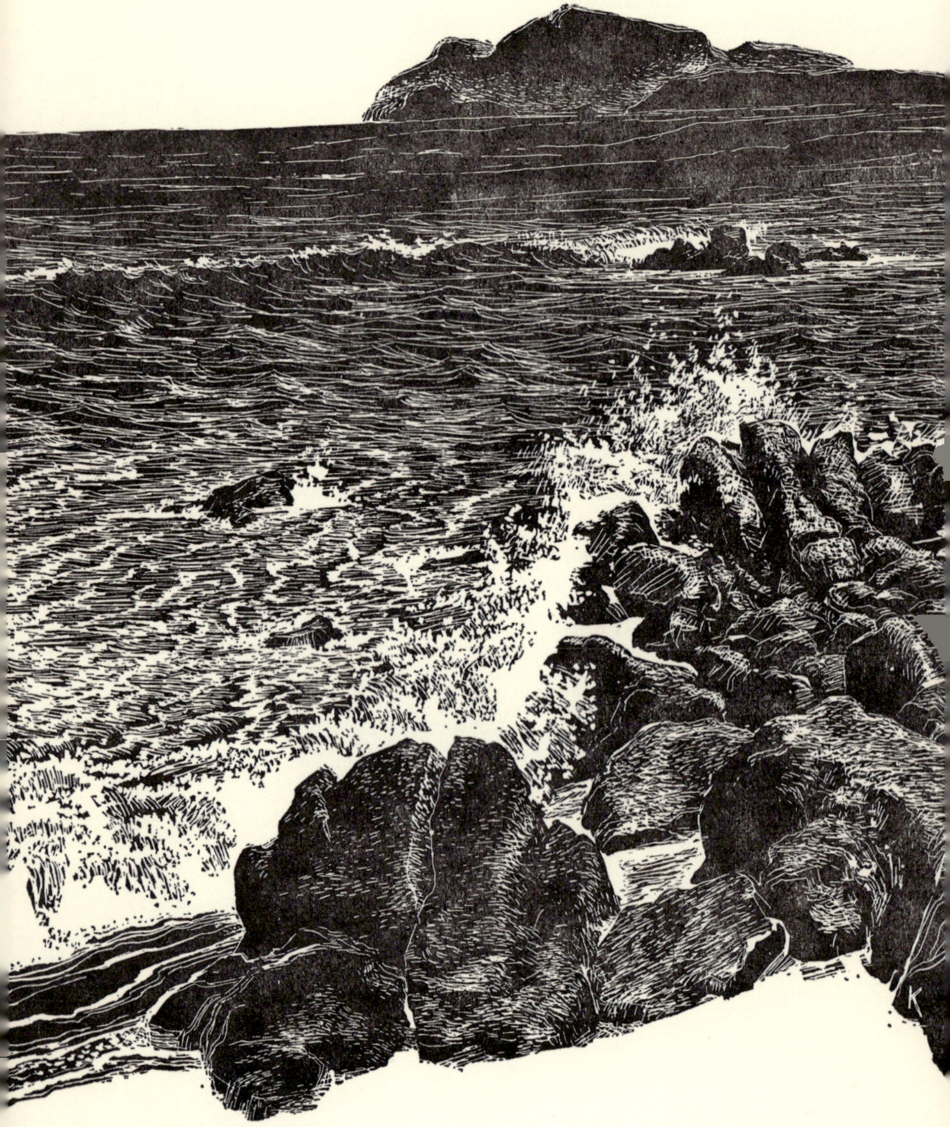

The Image

There is a blue horizon always
rising from the sea,
and a ship that is growing smaller,
disappearing into the sky,
and a gull
rising and falling
as waves rise and fall —
isolate, priestly,
as though attending
the God that goes with the wind.

The image is that of a man
going out of himself —
the ship bearing his body always ahead
while his mind returns to where he has been
and his heart follows the wind.

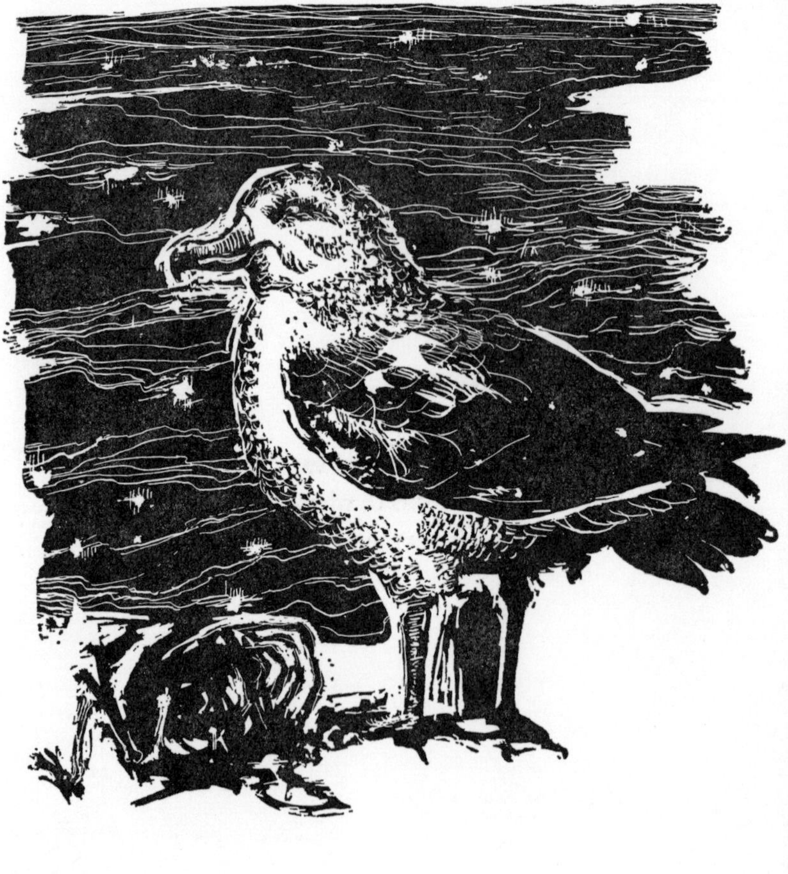

The Burglar

for Laura

the squawking, whining, scraping
breakfast of the gulls

startles you to waken
slide from the cocoon

of covers, gold and naked
shivering in the barred

sunlight through the window
you ask what that was

the roof is a boneyard
i say, our friends, the gulls

use it to crack the skulls
of clams, crabs, and snails

i thought it was a burglar
you say, i said it was

Petrels

they look like the birds
that service crocodiles

picking the sea's
enormous teeth

dust the waves
like butterflies

cut
blue dolls out of the air

their voices hardly
sound like the rain

more like crows
that catch the rain in their throats

The Foragers

Gulls have necks that move like worms
through the body of the air.

Balanced wings powered
by engines of the wind
they veer the wake for hours —

treasure-hunting garbage
dumped from the stern.

They prefer, as we, the visible —
the placenta of a ship
they gobble in the wake

to the fierce & picturesque
pursuit of silver fish.

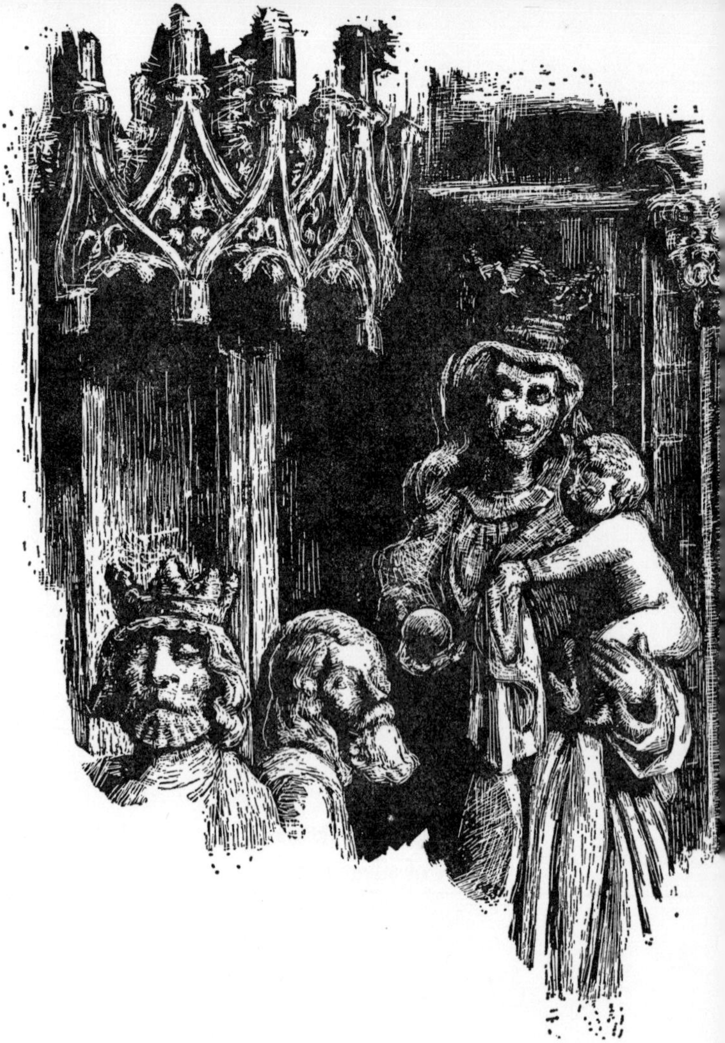

The Heir

I have seen the moon
hanging like a windbell
from the tallest tree in Tulsa.
The stars howled all night long.
The baby drags his diaper on the ground.
"What's there you like
about New York?
Jesus ... the smell's enough ..."
A girlfriend moaned in the backseat —
gnashing her teeth in the insulated dark
while dreams flew in and out of trees like bats.
The baby nags her breasts
that, loosened, protrude like hills
with blue trails.

....

"Jack's so much better-natured, now —
wait'll you see him!"
I see
the sores on the face of a child in Tangier
as I watch your baby suck, his cheeks
soft as the pouches of a squirrel —
eyes closed, like doors
to the throneroom of the world.

Memoirs

The trees in deserted Paris
On the Boulevard St. Germain
Stand recessed like huge vaginas
Sucking the August air.

O, all the *Parisiens* go down
Along the Mediterranean.
Then the *concierge* adores
Even *L'Americains*

(Vulgar as they are).
Comment allez-vous, Monsieur?
Très bien, we said, we said
Before we fled to bed —

That was so huge we both got lost
And never quite recovered.
I wonder if that bed still stands
With the *bidet* in the corner.

They seem so sensible, that race.
One can clean one's ass with grace
Before commenting on the worth
Of all the masters in the Louvre.

"Damned Frogs," we heard one jolly fellow
Say to his wife whose name was Mabel,
"Let's get the hell back to Alabama!"
We wished them well, and sat down at a table.

There is nothing like the breeze
That floats across the Seine
When you are sitting with your girl
And know it's going to rain.

Paris, I could write you our memoirs.
We no longer live together.
And when we try we can't quite ever
Separate the sweet from bitter.

So let us look through the *Bois de Boulogne,*
L'Orangerie, and the *Cimetière*
For two who simply loved one another.
They are there.

In the Osterreich

1

The wet wind wore us down,
shaggy clouds
scratching the sides of mountains,
flooding the Attersee —
clouds we watched
through the afternoons
when all we had to smoke was kef,
all to eat, sardines, and screwed,
and laughed at the old woman
listening in the next room —
clouds that ran like a pack of mongrels,
licking the marrow from our bones
noon after afternoon.

2

Nursing beers, we watched the workmen
drink May wine. With lifted voices
they sang what seemed to us school songs,
goosing one another between choruses;
growing sad at last.

3

When you came off the last bus from Salzburg
after three days . . . I couldn't speak
but nearly broke your back. You threw
yourself and all that lovely money
all over the bed. You were like my mother
twenty years before at the orphans home —
come back from the dead.

4

I'm sure those packs of clouds still run
over the mountains of the Attersee —
the water turning before the wind
blue and black and grey;
and in the yard our room looked over
the same old pregnant apple tree
drops its hard green bastards down.

December Letter to Nina

The Negro in my old room is sick
With the flu. I have it too.
Where did you say you were going to go?

They have called the Department of Public Health
Who advise that he don his uniform
Or the Doctor will not come.

Let's see, you said you would be back
Tomorrow — or was it the other day?
I am to meet you going the other way.

The hotel in Salzburg is cold. They want
The rent, and threaten to call the police.
You must be in line at American Express.

We don't spend *too* much time together.
It must be the Negro, or the Doctor.
What did you say that was the matter?

....

The weather's getting cold. Snow
piled up to the windowsill. I sit
and brood on what I know.

Snapshot

Cradling the Greek
    fisherman's sweater
as though it were a child, you sit
    surrounded by Dubrovnik.

The bay
    flows through your eyes.
Mountains
    grow out of your head.

You watch
    a few goats
herded by a crone
    straggle up the road.

You felt
    only disgust,
you said.
    The foetus was a mess.

Lake/Man/Bird

a sudden current
of air through reeds
and there it is
the lake   all alone
a huge belly of grey water
dawn

one thing receding before the next
hill on mountain   peak on peak
bird on the water   what
does that feeble
high-pitched cry
have to do with your life

this is all you will ever have
dawn   grey water   a lone swan
swimming in circles
feathers grey
as an old man's hair...

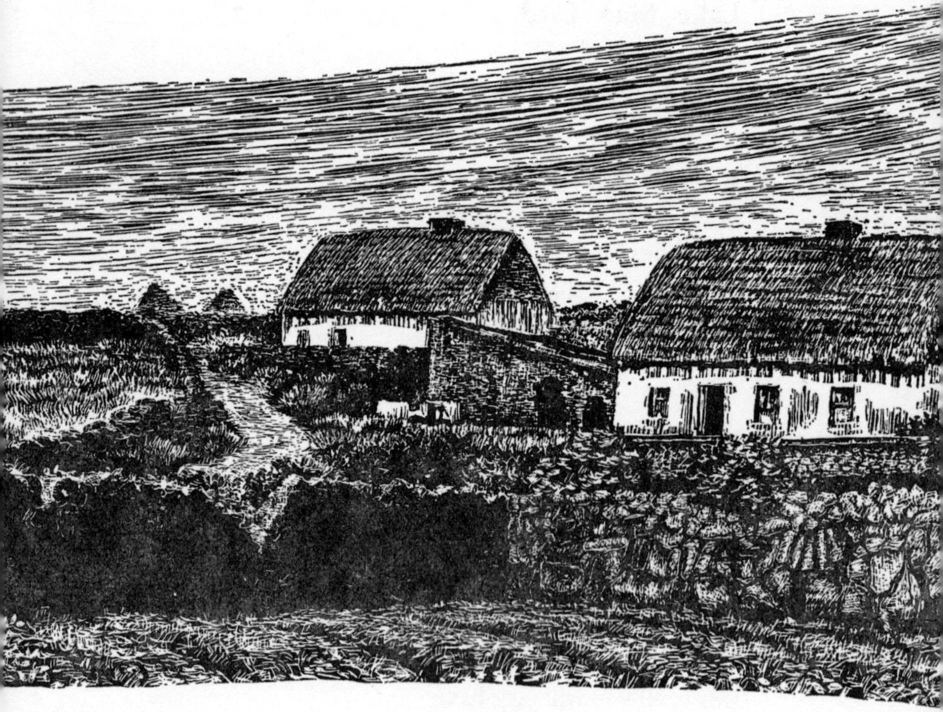

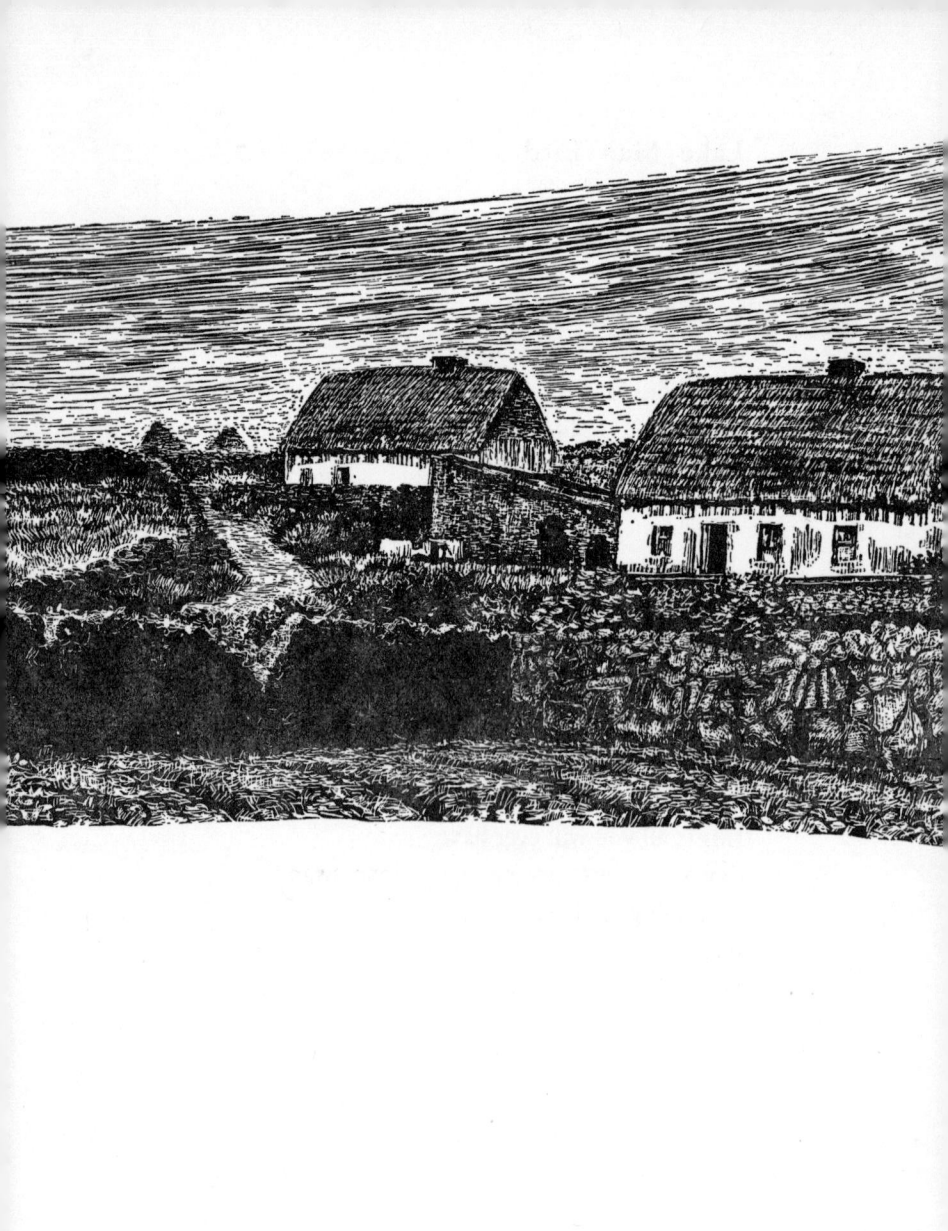

Poem for the People of Youghal

In a morning filled with silence
        and red clouds,
the bare street leading toward the sea,
moored boats rising with the tide,
hedgerowed hills dark green above the bay,
salmon fishers wrestling the waves,
wives snug in stone shacks,
        I ghost toward the harbor along
worn walls wet with dew.

Ireland's walls run dark and broken
        but the faces of children
color like the morning sky.
Their chattering could be the rooks
        whirling like black confetti
over the town at evening.

The tide slops over my boat like soup.
        Taut lines turn and yaw.
Sole, mottled black and brown,
thump in the stern, turn
        a cloudy eye on me before
the last quivered stiffening.

But I am dumb to fish reproach —
  the popping eye,
the flexing gills —
as are the salmon men
  who pull and haul the tide
with no more effort than the moon.

Icicles of light
  change to diamond fields.
The concave face of a cliff
and its huge shadow
  turn over like a windmill
with cloudy blades.

Flood tide is a stillness of the moon.
  Water makes a world of its own.
At the edge of the Gulf Stream
light lanes curve toward a buoy —
  red with a white stripe —
some whale-child's toy.

I gut the sixteen sole, one bass,
  and beach the boat.
The pailful of fish
set in a recess of the cliff,
  I climb.
My fingers turn to stone.

I think of men whose lives sound like the wind
      whipping along the cliffs,
whose heads
sink as low in stout as the hills in winter fog,
whose words tumble out of their mouths like birds —
cursing the bays and skies,
daydreaming of New York,
      Cousin Liam in Chicago,
two hundred dollars a week.